MAYER SMITH

Ravens of the Hidden Realm

Contents

One

The Raven's Call

L ira stood at the edge of the orchard, the cool wind tugging at the hem of her worn cloak, sending ripples across the grass. The trees, ancient and twisted, seemed to breathe with the rhythm of the land, their gnarled branches reaching for the heavens like skeletal hands. The sky, heavy with dark clouds, threatened rain. Yet it wasn't the storm she feared—it was the call of the raven.

It had been happening for days now. A soft, haunting cry that whispered to her from the deep corners of the forest, carried on the wind as though meant only for her ears. At first, she'd tried to ignore it, chalking it up to the strange pull of the changing season. But now, as the raven's song lingered in her thoughts, it gnawed at her, a sound she couldn't escape no matter how far she roamed.

Her heart quickened as another call echoed through the trees.

Kraaw!

A shiver ran down her spine, the noise like the scraping of a thousand bones. She turned, her eyes scanning the horizon, where the shadows of the forest seemed to stretch endlessly. There was no bird in sight, but she knew it wasn't an illusion. The raven had been close—too close for comfort.

She wrapped her arms around herself, a futile attempt to shield against the chill creeping into her bones. The village had warned her about the ravens; stories passed down through generations spoke of omens, curses, and shadowed secrets. Her grandmother had told her, in hushed tones, that the ravens had been born from the ancient magic that guarded the land—a magic so old it was lost to time, but never truly gone.

"Don't go near the woods, Lira," her grandmother had said with a sharp look in her eyes, "The ravens are always watching."

Lira pushed the memory aside. It was a cold night, and her grandmother's warnings felt distant and insignificant. The day had been quiet—too quiet—and the wind whispered like an unseen presence, urging her into the heart of the forest. It was only when she heard the call again, this time nearer, that she realized her feet had already begun to move.

Against her better judgment, she followed the sound.

The further she walked, the more the trees seemed to close in around her, their branches twisting into unsettling shapes, as though reaching for her. The sky above had darkened, the sun swallowed whole by a layer of thick, gray clouds. A drop of rain splashed against her cheek, followed by another. The air was thick with the scent of wet earth and pine, the fragrance of moss and decay.

Then, through the dense undergrowth, she saw it: a lone raven, perched on the edge of an ancient oak. Its feathers gleamed like midnight silk, and its beady eyes glinted with a knowing intelligence. The raven tilted its head, staring at her with a curiosity that unsettled her more than it should have.

She froze, her pulse hammering in her throat. There was something unnerving about the way it watched her, as if it could see into her soul. Her grandmother had been right— ravens were never just birds. They were watchers, messengers of fate.

Suddenly, the raven cawed, the sound sharp and demanding. Lira's breath caught in her throat. It wasn't the call of a wild bird; it was too deliberate, too intent. The raven's wings fluttered, and it took flight, rising into the sky with an ease that made Lira's heart race. But it didn't fly away. No, it circled, slowly at first, then faster, as if beckoning her.

Her feet moved before she could stop them, following the raven deeper into the forest. The trees parted as if allowing her passage, and she found herself in a small clearing bathed in a strange, pale light. The air was still, the oppressive weight of the storm above suspended in a heavy silence. The raven landed on a stone slab in the center of the clearing, its eyes never leaving hers.

Lira's breath quickened. Something was wrong here—something in the air, in the way the raven watched her, in the way the trees seemed to breathe around her. She couldn't explain it, but the forest felt… alive, aware.

"Why are you following me?" she whispered to the bird, her voice trembling. But of course, it didn't answer. It never did. Instead, it tilted its head once more, almost in curiosity.

Then, a rustle behind her. She spun, her heart leaping into her throat.

From the shadows, a figure emerged—tall, cloaked in darkness, moving with the silent grace of a predator. His presence felt like a disruption in the very air, a shift that sent a fresh chill through her bones.

"Did you hear it too?" The voice was low, almost a growl, thick with an accent she couldn't place. The man stepped into the clearing, his face hidden beneath the hood of his cloak. His gaze, however, was sharp, piercing, and locked onto her with an intensity that sent a shiver running down her spine.

The raven fluttered its wings, as though reacting to his presence, and took flight, vanishing into the storm-heavy sky.

Lira stood frozen, her mouth dry. "Who are you?"

The stranger didn't answer right away. His eyes, the color of storm clouds, searched her face, as though deciding something. His hands, hidden in the folds of his cloak, clenched and unclenched.

"I should be asking you that," he said, his voice edged with both caution and something else—something far more dangerous. "You're here, in the woods. Following the raven."

Lira's stomach dropped. "You were following it too."

"I've been tracking it for days," he replied, stepping closer. "It's never led me this far before."

The tension between them crackled like electricity, and despite herself, Lira took a step back. "What do you want with the raven?"

The man's gaze flickered, a brief flash of something unreadable in his eyes. "I need something from it. Something that's tied to these woods. To the land itself."

She frowned. "What are you talking about?"

His gaze softened, just a little. "I'm not here to harm you."

But she wasn't so sure. There was a certain danger in his presence, something that made her feel both drawn to him and repelled at the same time.

"I don't know why I'm here," Lira admitted, her voice quiet, almost lost beneath the rising wind. "The raven… it calls to me. It's like it knows me. Like it's pulling me toward something." She paused, feeling a strange heaviness in her chest, as if her words had opened a door she couldn't close again. "I don't understand."

The man's expression softened, and for a moment, he almost seemed… sympathetic. He took another step forward, lowering his hood. His face was striking, sharp angles and a ruggedness that belonged to someone who had lived a thousand lives. His hair was dark, nearly black, and his jaw was covered in a light stubble that only accentuated the hardness of his features.

"You're not the only one who feels it," he murmured, his voice barely audible above the wind. "But you're the first to come this close."

The raven's call echoed again, distant now, but still unmistakable. Kraaw!

Lira's heart skipped a beat. Something had changed in the air— something ancient, something that couldn't be ignored. The forest, the raven, the stranger—everything was connected. But how? And why her?

The man's eyes flickered toward the horizon, his jaw tightening. "It's starting."

Lira had no idea what he meant, but she felt it deep in her gut. The storm was coming.

And it would change everything.

Two

Whispers in the Woods

The storm hadn't quite broken by the time Lira made her way back through the forest, her feet crunching against the wet leaves, a rhythmic, almost hypnotic sound beneath the steady patter of rain. She had walked the path back to the village before—this narrow, moss-covered trail that wound its way between towering oaks and sprawling ferns—but tonight, the forest felt unfamiliar. The air was too thick, too heavy, as though the trees themselves were holding their breath.

Lira pulled her cloak tighter around her shoulders, the fabric damp from the rain but providing some comfort in the oppressive silence. The call of the raven still echoed in her mind, a low hum that had taken residence in her thoughts. She couldn't shake it, no matter how hard she tried.

Behind her, the figure of the man—the stranger—lingered in her thoughts, his piercing eyes, his quiet voice, his presence as unsettling as it was magnetic. She couldn't understand why he had been there, or why she had felt so drawn to him, even as a part of her recoiled from the intensity of his gaze.

"Focus, Lira," she whispered to herself, hoping the words would steady her. "Just get back to the village."

But even as she spoke, she felt a pull deeper into the forest, as though the woods themselves were calling her. A strange energy hummed beneath the surface of the earth, alive with something ancient and waiting.

Suddenly, a low growl echoed through the trees.

Lira froze. Her breath caught in her throat. The sound wasn't like any animal she knew. It was deep, resonating, and oddly human. Her heart pounded, every instinct telling her to run. But she didn't move. She couldn't.

The growl came again, closer this time, followed by a faint rustling in the underbrush. A shadow flitted between the trees, too quick to fully see but unmistakably there. Lira's pulse spiked. She wasn't alone in the woods.

A figure emerged from the darkness—tall, cloaked, moving with a fluid grace that made him appear part of the forest itself. She didn't need to look up to know it was him. The same stranger from the clearing. The same dangerous pull she had felt earlier.

"Why are you following me?" she asked, her voice trembling despite her best efforts to remain composed.

He didn't answer right away. Instead, his eyes scanned the surrounding trees, his expression unreadable. There was a flash of something in his gaze, something like recognition—or maybe warning.

"You shouldn't be here alone," he said, his voice a low rumble, thick with an accent that was difficult to place.

Lira took a step back, her body instinctively recoiling, even though the stranger hadn't moved toward her. "I'm fine. I can handle myself."

His lips twisted into a half-smile, a smile that didn't reach his eyes. "The woods don't care about what you can handle."

She swallowed hard. His words made her feel exposed, as though everything she thought she understood about this place was a lie.

"You didn't answer my question," she pressed, her voice stronger now, though it still quivered. "Why are you following me?"

The man stepped closer, his boots silent on the wet earth. There was a tension in the way he moved, a predator's grace. "Because you're not supposed to be out here alone," he said, his voice soft but firm. "The raven brought you here. And when the raven calls, there are things in these woods you don't want to meet."

Lira's heart stuttered in her chest. The raven brought me here. The words echoed in her mind. Had he seen the same pull she had felt? Could he hear the call too? She looked up at him, trying to steady her breath. "I don't understand. What does it want from me?"

He studied her for a moment, his eyes dark like storm clouds, unreadable. Then, he leaned in, his voice a low whisper. "It's not about what it wants from you, Lira. It's what you're meant to do."

Her breath caught in her throat. "What I'm meant to do?"

The man didn't respond immediately, his gaze shifting briefly to the woods around them. The wind had picked up, the branches of the trees groaning under the strain of the coming storm. But it wasn't just the weather. There was a palpable sense of danger in the air, a shift that made the hairs on the back of Lira's neck stand on end.

"I've been watching you," he said, his voice barely audible over the wind. "For a long time. Ever since the first call."

Lira blinked, her pulse quickening. "What are you talking about? Who are you?"

His lips parted, as if about to speak, but then something changed in his expression—something he had been trying to keep hidden slipped to the surface. There was a flicker of something too personal, too intense in his eyes, and Lira felt a strange warmth spread through her chest. It was more than attraction. It was as if a door had opened, and something ancient and deeply tied to her own soul had beckoned her through.

"I don't know why the raven is calling you," he said, his voice rougher now. "But I know this: there's more to this place than you understand. And you're not the first to be pulled in."

Lira took a step back, her mind reeling. "What do you mean? What's going on in these woods?"

He looked at her for a long moment, his gaze softening for the briefest of moments before hardening again. "There are forces here. Old forces. And you're part of it. You're part of something that's been buried for centuries."

The air between them seemed to thicken, the words heavy with meaning. Lira didn't know what to say. The weight of his words settled on her shoulders, the realization creeping in like a fog. Something about this man, this stranger, felt far more familiar than she wanted to admit. It was as if their meeting had been written in the stars—no, more than that. It felt as if they had always been destined to meet in this moment, in this very place.

The man took a step forward, his gaze never leaving hers. "You need to leave, Lira. Now. Before it's too late."

But she didn't move. The urge to understand—to know—kept her rooted to the spot. "I can't leave. Not yet. Not when I don't understand what's happening. When you won't even tell me who you are."

The stranger's eyes flashed with something sharp, almost pained. "It's not safe for you to know everything. Not yet." He paused, as though weighing something. "My name is Thorne. And I'm here to make sure you survive what's coming."

Thorne. The name settled in her mind like the sound of the raven's call—familiar, yet haunting.

"Survive?" Lira echoed. "What's coming?"

Thorne's gaze flickered toward the darkening trees. The wind howled in the distance, the storm now nearly upon them. "You've already started something," he said, his voice tight with urgency. "And once the raven's call has been answered, there's no turning back."

Before Lira could respond, Thorne stepped away, his figure disappearing into the shadows of the trees with a swift, almost ethereal grace. She stood there for a long moment, her heart racing, the air around her charged with electricity. The raven's call still echoed through the forest, louder now, as if waiting for something.

As if waiting for her.

Three

The Unseen Hand

Lira's feet brushed over the wet earth as she walked back to her cottage, her thoughts clouded with a mixture of confusion, fear, and something she couldn't quite place—something that curled in her chest whenever she thought of Thorne. His name seemed to linger in the air, heavy and weighty, like the scent of rain on the wind, and with it came a pull she couldn't resist. Even now, she could feel it—a magnetic force drawing her toward him, a force she didn't fully understand but couldn't deny.

The forest was still and quiet around her, but the silence was unnerving, thick with an oppressive sense of anticipation. The rain had stopped, leaving behind a damp mist that hung in the air, clinging to the trees like a second skin. The once familiar trail now seemed strange, even alien, as though the woods had shifted since the moment she had stepped into them that night.

With every step, she could hear the rustling of leaves, the snap of twigs beneath her boots, but it felt as though someone—something—was following her. The hairs on the back of her neck stood up, and she had to fight the overwhelming urge to look over her shoulder.

And then, just as her cottage came into view, a whisper caught on the wind.

"Lira…"

Her heart skipped, and she froze, her breath caught in her throat. The voice was low, intimate, and unmistakable—Thorne. It wasn't just in her head; it was as if the trees themselves had carried his words to her.

She spun around, but the woods were empty, the mist swirling around her like a ghostly veil. No figure, no shadow—nothing.

The silence grew deafening, but the sensation of being watched remained, creeping under her skin like a chill that refused to leave.

"Stop it," she whispered, shaking her head as she pressed forward toward her cottage, her pulse quickening. "It's just the forest playing tricks."

But even as she muttered those words, she knew they weren't true. The forest hadn't changed—it was her perception of it that had shifted. Since meeting Thorne, since stepping deeper into this mysterious world, everything felt different. The world felt…alive, alive in ways she hadn't understood before.

She reached the door of her cottage, her fingers trembling as she grasped the wooden handle. But as she opened it, a cold draft swept out, sending a shiver down her spine. The fire in the hearth had gone out, the room darker than it should have been.

The soft sound of breathing broke the stillness.

Lira's heart slammed against her ribs as her eyes darted to the far corner of the room. There, seated by the cold hearth, was a figure she hadn't expected to see. Thorne. His presence filled the room with an almost palpable tension, his silhouette sharp against the dim light of the room. His coat, dark as night, was soaked through with rain, his hair wet and clinging to his forehead.

"You," she breathed, her voice a mixture of disbelief and something else—something raw, almost desperate.

Thorne didn't move, didn't speak at first. His gaze, however, never left her. It was intense, like he could see into every part of her. His eyes, stormy and deep, seemed to search her soul, peeling back every layer of defense she had ever built.

"You shouldn't be here," she said, her voice shaking. "How did you find me?"

"I wasn't looking for you," Thorne replied, his voice like gravel, deep and low. "But I couldn't stay away."

Lira swallowed hard, her throat dry. A strange flutter moved in her chest at his words—an echo of something long buried, a recognition that chilled her to the bone.

He stood then, slowly, deliberately, as though he didn't want to startle her. His boots creaked softly against the wooden floor, the sound like a whisper of warning.

"Why are you here?" she asked, her voice barely above a whisper.

Thorne took a step toward her, his eyes never leaving hers. "Because I need to warn you."

"Warn me?" she repeated, her heart beating faster. "Warn me about what?"

He didn't answer right away. Instead, his eyes flickered toward the window, where the trees outside seemed to sway, their dark limbs twisting and turning, as if they were alive, reaching for something.

"The ravens," Thorne murmured. "They've been watching you."

Lira's stomach dropped, and she took an instinctive step back, her back meeting the doorframe. The cold draft from the night outside wrapped around her, biting at her skin. The fire had long since died, but the coldness in the room felt far more suffocating than the chill of the storm.

"I told you already," she said, her voice hardening. "I don't want to be part of whatever this is. Whatever game you're playing." She shook her head, trying to regain control of her racing thoughts. "I just want to live my life."

"You can't," Thorne replied, his voice unyielding. "Not any-more."

Lira's breath caught in her chest, and she stepped away from the door, though it felt like the walls themselves were closing in around her. "What do you mean?"

He didn't answer immediately, but the look on his face—a mixture of frustration and something deeper, more troubled—told her he wasn't going to make this easy.

"The raven," he began, his voice soft, almost reverent, "isn't just a bird. It's a messenger, a harbinger. And it's been calling to you, Lira. I have been following it for a long time."

She shook her head, taking another step back. "I don't under-stand."

Thorne's eyes softened for a moment, and he stepped closer, his presence overwhelming, suffocating. He was right there now, close enough that she could feel the heat of his body, the dampness of his coat seeping into the air around them. His scent—earth and rain—invaded her senses, sending a wave of dizziness through her.

"You will understand," he said, his voice almost a promise. "But first, you need to know something. There's more going on here than just the ravens. More than just the forest. Something is waking up, something dark, something ancient. And you're part of it, whether you want to be or not."

Lira stared at him, her mind racing to catch up with his words, but the fear in her chest only grew. She could feel it now, the weight of the unseen hand he spoke of—the force that had been stirring beneath the surface of her life, pulling at the threads of her existence like some invisible puppeteer.

"I don't want to be part of this," she whispered, her voice trembling despite herself. "I don't want to be a part of whatever this is."

Thorne took a deep breath, his eyes flickering with something between sympathy and regret. He reached out, his hand brushing against hers in a touch that was electric, almost painful. For a moment, the room felt impossibly still.

"You don't have a choice," he said softly. "You're already in it."

Lira's breath caught in her throat, and before she could respond, a sharp, unsettling caw echoed from the window. The sound was unmistakable.

The raven.

Thorne's eyes darkened, his grip on her hand tightening just a fraction. "It's too late. The ravens have made their choice."

Outside, the wind howled, and the storm broke with a violent crack of thunder.

And everything began to change.

Four

The Raven's Curse

The storm had come with a vengeance, battering the land with its relentless fury. Rain poured down in sheets, turning the world outside Lira's cottage into a blur of darkened silhouettes and shadows. The wind screamed through the trees, howling like a living creature, and the occasional crack of thunder shook the very foundation of the earth beneath her feet. But inside, the atmosphere was still, thick with the tension that had been building since Thorne's arrival.

Lira sat at the small wooden table, her fingers absently tracing the edge of her cup, watching the steam curl upward like the smoke of an ancient fire. Her thoughts were a tangled mess, each one more unsettling than the last. The raven's call. Thorne's words. The weight of something hidden beneath the surface of her life, something she could not understand but could no longer ignore.

She had thought that by closing herself off from the world, she could escape whatever dark forces lurked in the shadows of the woods. But the storm outside was not the only thing that had been stirring. She felt the darkness inching closer, felt it pressing in on her from all sides, just beyond her reach. The raven had chosen her, and now she couldn't escape it. The truth, whatever it was, was closing in, and she was helpless to stop it.

A knock on the door broke through the quiet, startling her from her thoughts. She didn't need to turn to know it was Thorne. No one else would come out here in this weather. Her chest tightened at the thought of him. She had told herself she didn't want him here, but every part of her longed for his presence, even as she resented it. There was something magnetic about him, something that both terrified and thrilled her. His eyes, stormy and intense, seemed to reach into her very soul, dragging out emotions she wasn't ready to face.

She stood slowly, her legs unsteady, and crossed to the door. Her heart pounded in her chest, and she couldn't quite explain why. The silence before opening it felt like an eternity, but when she finally pulled the door open, Thorne was standing there, drenched from the rain. His cloak was dark with moisture, clinging to his body, and his hair, damp and wild, framed his face in a way that made him seem even more dangerous, more mysterious than before.

The cold night air rushed in with him, and for a brief moment, they simply stood there, the world outside forgotten as the air between them seemed to pulse with tension.

"Lira," Thorne said, his voice low and gravelly, a hint of something urgent beneath the calm facade. His eyes flickered over her, searching for something he didn't say. "You shouldn't be here alone."

She couldn't stop herself from meeting his gaze, and for a long moment, it felt like time had stopped. She swallowed hard, her pulse quickening. "I'm fine," she said, her voice too soft, too unsure. "I don't need you to—"

But Thorne stepped inside before she could finish, his movement swift and decisive, like he had already made up his mind. His presence filled the small space, crowding her, and for a moment, Lira couldn't breathe. She took a step back, trying to put some distance between them, but it didn't help. The air was thick, charged with something she couldn't name, and it made her feel exposed, vulnerable, in a way she had never felt before.

Thorne closed the door behind him, his eyes still fixed on her. "You're not fine, Lira." His voice was sharp, insistent, and it made her heart beat faster. "You've been hearing the raven's call. I know you have. I've felt it too."

Lira's breath caught in her throat, and her eyes widened. She opened her mouth to say something, but the words wouldn't come. She had thought she was the only one, that somehow, the pull of the raven was hers and hers alone. But Thorne's words shattered that illusion, and the truth hit her with a force she wasn't prepared for.

"What do you mean?" she finally managed to say, her voice

barely more than a whisper.

Thorne took a step closer, his eyes softening just a fraction. "I mean that you're part of something much larger than you realize. Something ancient. The ravens… they don't choose just anyone." He paused, his gaze lingering on her face, as if searching for the right words. "They chose you, Lira. And with that choice comes a curse."

Lira shook her head, her mind spinning. A curse? It was too much to grasp. "I don't believe in curses," she said, more firmly than she felt. "I don't—"

"Then why do you feel it?" Thorne's voice was soft, almost a challenge, but there was something in his eyes that made her pause. "Why does your heart race every time you hear it? Why does your skin prickle with each call, as if it's reaching inside of you, pulling something out?"

Lira closed her eyes, her fingers clenching into fists at her sides. She didn't want to admit it, didn't want to acknowledge the truth that had been lingering at the edges of her mind for days. But he was right. The raven's call had been more than just a sound. It had been a summons, a pull that had led her to the heart of the woods, to the place where something else was waiting.

"Why me?" she whispered, her voice barely audible, as if saying the words out loud would make it all too real.

Thorne's expression softened, but there was still something

dark behind his eyes, something that spoke of dangers she couldn't understand. He reached out, his hand hovering near her cheek, as if unsure whether he had the right to touch her.

"You have no choice in this," he said softly. "Once the raven's call is answered, you're bound to it. And whatever it is—whatever it wants—you can't escape it."

Lira's heart raced. "What do you mean? What does the raven want from me?"

"I don't know yet," Thorne admitted, his voice low. "But I intend to find out. There's something here, something ancient and powerful, and it's waking up. And the raven is the key. It's always been the key."

She could feel the weight of his words, their implications settling heavily in the pit of her stomach. It was impossible, yet undeniable. The raven, the forest, Thorne—they were all part of something she had never imagined, something far more dangerous and complicated than she had ever wanted to believe.

The air around them crackled, the storm outside seeming to mirror the storm that raged within her. There was so much she didn't know, so much that Thorne wasn't telling her. Yet, in the depths of her heart, she felt an undeniable pull toward him. Despite everything—despite the fear, despite the danger—she wanted to trust him.

Thorne stepped closer, his voice barely a whisper now. "Lira... I know this isn't what you wanted. I know you didn't ask for this.

But you're not alone in this. I'll help you. I'll protect you."

Lira's breath caught in her throat as she looked into his eyes. They were so intense, so full of things unsaid, and for a moment, she saw the vulnerability there, something raw and unspoken. Something that called to her.

She nodded slowly, her voice trembling as she said, "Okay. I'll trust you. But I need to know the truth. All of it."

Thorne didn't say anything for a long moment, his gaze never leaving hers. Finally, he nodded. "You will. But first…" He reached into his coat, pulling out a small, worn book. The cover was old, faded, the edges frayed from years of use. "This is where it begins. And this is where it will end."

Lira took the book from him, her hands trembling. She opened it carefully, the pages yellowed with age, and the strange symbols written within seemed to pulse with an energy she couldn't understand.

And in that moment, she realized: there was no going back.

Into the Hidden Realm

Lira's fingers trembled as she traced the worn symbols etched into the pages of the ancient book Thorne had handed her. The scent of aged paper and ink filled the room, mingling with the dampness of the storm outside. The fire in the hearth sputtered, casting flickering shadows that danced across the walls like twisted specters. It felt as though the very air had changed, thick with something that was both otherworldly and familiar.

Thorne stood across from her, his eyes fixed on her as she read, as if he were waiting for her to decipher the mysteries hidden within the cryptic words. The room was silent except for the occasional crackle of the fire and the soft sound of the rain pelting against the windows. Lira's heartbeat thrummed in her ears, louder than the storm, as she flipped through the pages, each one revealing more about the dark forces tied to her bloodline, more about the curse she could no longer ignore.

Her gaze lifted from the book to meet Thorne's, and for a moment, the storm outside seemed to fade. His eyes were dark, filled with something unreadable, something that both unsettled and drew her in. He was standing in the dim light of the room, his coat still wet from the rain, his presence as commanding as the force that had led her into this world.

"I don't understand," she whispered, her voice raw with uncertainty. "These symbols—they don't make any sense. What are they? What's happening to me?"

Thorne stepped closer, the heat of his body radiating toward her, and his gaze softened, though there was still an underlying tension, like a storm about to break. "The symbols are part of an ancient language. A language of power, of magic. They're the key to understanding what's happening to you, to the raven's call. They were written long ago, by those who lived before us—those who had the knowledge to control the forces of the realm."

Lira swallowed, her fingers gripping the edges of the book tighter. "But I don't want any of this. I never asked for any of this." Her voice shook as she spoke, the weight of the truth sinking in like a stone in her chest. "Why me? Why did the raven choose me?"

Thorne's gaze darkened, and he took a slow step forward, his boots scraping lightly against the wooden floor. "I don't know," he said, his voice thick with regret. "But I think you do, deep down. The raven's call—it's not random. It's tied to you, to your bloodline. And it's been calling for centuries."

Lira's breath caught in her throat, the air suddenly heavy with something ancient and powerful. The words hung in the space between them, unanswered questions swirling in the room like a storm cloud. She could feel it now, more than ever—the pull of something beyond her control. Something darker, older than anything she had ever imagined.

"Your family…" Thorne began, but his voice faltered for a moment. He seemed to hesitate, as if deciding how much to reveal. "Your bloodline is cursed, Lira. The curse has been passed down through generations, and it has always been tied to the ravens."

Lira's heart skipped a beat, the air around her suddenly charged with electricity. "A curse? You're telling me this… this curse has been following my family? All this time?"

Thorne nodded, his eyes never leaving hers. "The raven is the key, and you…" He paused, his voice dropping to a whisper. "You're the one who will break it—or bind it forever."

Lira's breath caught in her throat, her pulse quickening. "What do you mean? How can I break it? How can I—"

Before she could finish, the room seemed to shift, the temperature plummeting. A gust of wind howled through the cracks in the door, and the flames in the hearth flickered wildly. The book in Lira's hands fluttered, as if it were alive, its pages turning rapidly as if some unseen force were controlling them.

Thorne's eyes narrowed, his hand reaching out to steady the book, his fingers brushing against hers in the process. The touch sent a jolt of warmth through her, despite the cold in the air, and she could feel the weight of his gaze pressing down on her.

"It's happening," Thorne said, his voice low, almost a growl. "It's calling to you. The raven is drawing you in. And soon, the veil between this world and the hidden realm will open."

Lira could barely catch her breath, the words swirling around her like the wind outside. The hidden realm. The words sounded ancient, like they belonged to a forgotten time, and yet they held a power that made her blood run cold.

"What do you mean 'the veil'?" she whispered, her voice trembling. "What hidden realm?"

Thorne didn't answer immediately. His eyes were fixed on her, and for a moment, Lira thought he wasn't going to say anything. Then, slowly, he spoke, his voice heavy with something she couldn't quite understand.

"The hidden realm is where the magic comes from. It's a place that exists just beyond the edges of our reality. A place where the forces that govern life and death, light and dark, are balanced. But the veil between our world and theirs is thin—and when the raven calls, it's a sign that the balance is shifting. That the barrier is weakening. And you, Lira, are the key."

Lira's heart raced. "I don't understand. How am I the key? I don't even know what this is. I don't know what's happening to me."

Thorne's eyes softened, and for a moment, he seemed to struggle with the words. "You don't remember, do you?" he asked softly, his voice almost tender. "The night of the storm. The night you were born. The raven's call was there, Lira. It marked you. And it's been watching, waiting, for the right moment."

Lira's mind reeled, her thoughts tumbling over each other. The storm. The raven. The pull that had always been there, just beyond her reach. Was it all connected?

"Tonight," Thorne continued, his voice low and urgent, "the veil will open. The hidden realm will bleed into this one, and we won't be able to stop it. The curse will claim you—or you will have to claim it."

Lira's chest tightened, her heart hammering in her chest as she looked at him. The storm outside raged louder now, as though the very world were reacting to Thorne's words. The wind howled through the trees, and the sound of the raven's call pierced the air, sharp and clear.

The raven's call.

Lira's breath caught in her throat as the realization hit her like a blow to the chest. "I am the key." Her voice cracked as she said it aloud. The weight of it settled heavily on her shoulders, and her world tilted. "What am I supposed to do? How can I break it? How can I stop this?"

Thorne stepped closer, his eyes never leaving hers. There was something in his gaze—something raw, something desperate—that made her stomach flip. "I don't know, Lira," he admitted softly, his voice barely above a whisper. "But we have to go. Now."

Lira hesitated, her mind a whirlwind of thoughts, but something in Thorne's voice—something in the urgency of his words—told her she didn't have a choice. The veil was opening, and she had no idea what waited on the other side.

The storm outside seemed to roar in response, a final, deafening call to action. Thorne took her hand then, his grip firm and warm, and for a moment, Lira felt that strange connection between them—something deep and undeniable, like two souls that had been entwined for lifetimes.

"Come with me, Lira," Thorne said, his voice both pleading and commanding. "We're running out of time."

Lira nodded, her heart pounding in her chest as she took a step toward him. She didn't know where they were going, but in that moment, it didn't matter. All that mattered was that they were in this together—and whatever happened next, she would face it with him by her side.

Together, they stepped into the storm.

Six

The Heart of the Raven

The storm raged around them, the wind shrieking through the trees, whipping their wet cloaks around them like ghostly specters. Lira could barely hear Thorne's voice over the fury of the tempest, but she knew he was speaking to her—his words cutting through the howling chaos with an urgency that sent a tremor of fear through her chest.

"Stay close," Thorne said, his voice sharp and commanding. "The veil is thin, and it's not safe out here. We have to move quickly."

Lira nodded, though the words felt distant, lost in the noise of the world around them. Her heart pounded in her chest, the rhythm of her pulse matching the wild beat of the storm. She was cold—colder than she had ever been—and yet, she felt an overwhelming sense of heat coming from Thorne, as though his presence could somehow shield her from the forces beyond her comprehension. The raven's call still echoed in her mind, sharp and relentless, a sound that seemed to reach into her very bones.

They moved through the forest at a fast pace, their feet slipping on the slick earth, the path winding like a dark ribbon through the trees. The rain continued to pour, drenching them, but Lira barely noticed the cold now. The air had thickened with something more than the storm. The very ground beneath her feet seemed to pulse with an energy she couldn't explain. Every step took her deeper into the unknown, further from everything she had known, and closer to the heart of something ancient and powerful.

The trees around them seemed to shift, their trunks groaning under the strain of the storm, their branches twisting unnaturally, as though they were alive. Lira's skin prickled with an uneasy awareness, and her breath quickened as the air around her thickened. It felt as though the very forest was watching her—waiting.

She reached out instinctively, her fingers brushing against the bark of one of the massive trees. The wood was smooth, too smooth, and her fingers stung as if the tree itself were alive. A soft, almost imperceptible hum vibrated through the ground, and Lira staggered back, a gasp escaping her lips.

Thorne turned sharply, his gaze locking onto her. There was something in his eyes—something too intense to read—but it made Lira's heart skip a beat. His jaw tightened as he reached out, his hand brushing hers for the briefest moment. His touch was electric, like a spark igniting a fire deep within her.

"Don't touch it," he said softly, his voice low and urgent. "It's part of the barrier. The closer we get to the heart of it, the more the magic will pull at you. You have to stay focused."

Lira nodded, though her mind felt clouded. There was something in the air, something ancient, something alive, and it called to her. She could feel the pull of it, deep within her bones, as though the forest itself had become a part of her.

They continued forward, the trees growing denser as they moved deeper into the heart of the woods. The shadows between the trees stretched like dark fingers, the air thick with the scent of damp earth and decay. The moon was obscured by the storm clouds, casting everything into an unnatural, heavy darkness.

Thorne led her forward, his movements sure and steady, his grip firm on her hand as if to reassure her, though she knew neither of them were certain of what lay ahead. There was an undeniable tension between them, a crackling awareness that neither of them could ignore. The storm outside raged, but the air between them felt charged—thick with an intensity that neither the rain nor the wind could quell.

"You're the key, Lira," Thorne said, his voice barely a whisper, though it seemed to cut through the storm. "This… whatever is happening… it's tied to you. To your bloodline. The raven isn't just calling you—it's pulling you into this. You were always meant to be part of it."

Her heart skipped a beat at his words, and she looked at him, her breath catching in her throat. She had always felt different, always sensed that there was more to her story than she could ever understand. But this… this was something entirely new. Something she hadn't been prepared for. She could feel the weight of his words settling in her chest, and they clung to her like the coldness of the storm.

"I never asked for any of this," she said, her voice trembling despite herself. "I just… I just want to live a normal life. I don't understand why I'm the one… why me?"

Thorne's grip tightened, his thumb brushing over her knuckles in a gesture that should have been comforting but only made her feel more exposed. "I don't know, Lira," he said quietly. "But the answers are here, in the heart of the forest. We'll find them together."

His words, though reassuring, didn't quite reach her heart. There was too much uncertainty in them, too much unspoken fear in the way he held her. She wasn't sure if it was for her safety or his own. His eyes—those stormy eyes—were dark with something, something she didn't fully understand.

The path before them seemed to twist, the trees leaning inward, as if guiding them toward something. The ground beneath her feet had become slick with rain and mud, and the wind howled like a wolf on the hunt. Yet, despite the storm's fury, there was something strangely quiet about the air around them, as though the world had fallen still, waiting.

They reached a clearing, and as they stepped into it, Lira felt a shift—a moment of stillness that clung to the air. The rain seemed to cease, the wind dying down to a mere whisper. The clearing was bathed in an eerie, pale light, though the moon remained hidden behind the clouds.

In the center of the clearing stood an ancient stone altar, covered in vines and moss, weathered by time. The stone was cold, almost lifeless, but Lira could feel the pulse of energy coming from it. The raven's call was louder here, more insistent, as if the sound itself was the heartbeat of the forest.

Thorne stopped, his breath quickening, his eyes narrowed as he looked toward the altar. "This is it," he said, his voice low and tense. "This is where it began."

Lira felt a strange, undeniable pull toward the altar, as if the very earth beneath her feet was guiding her. Her breath caught in her throat as her gaze fell on the carvings etched into the stone. They were ancient symbols, just like the ones in the book, but there was something more here—something deeper, darker.

"The raven is the key," Thorne said, his voice hoarse. "And you… you're the one who must unlock it."

Lira's heart raced, her mind spinning with questions, with fear, with an impossible desire to understand. She didn't want to be part of this. She didn't want to be the one tied to something so dark, so ancient. But the pull was too strong, and she found herself taking a step toward the altar, unable to stop herself.

Thorne's hand shot out, grabbing her wrist just as she reached the stone. His grip was tight, almost painful, and his eyes locked onto hers with an intensity that made her breath catch in her chest.

"Don't," he whispered, his voice strained. "You don't understand what you're about to do."

Lira's chest tightened, her breath shallow as she looked up at him. The words were on the tip of her tongue—What do I do? How do I stop this?—but they didn't come. Instead, she found herself staring into Thorne's eyes, searching for something. Answers. Assurance. Anything.

And for the briefest of moments, she saw something flicker there—something soft.

Then, without warning, the air around them seemed to snap. The ground trembled beneath her feet, the air crackling with energy, and a single raven soared down from the sky, its wings beating powerfully through the storm, its eyes locked on her.

It was time.

Seven

Betrayal in the Dark

The wind had shifted again, sweeping through the trees with a low, mournful howl that felt almost like a warning. Lira stood at the edge of the clearing, her breath shallow, her hands trembling slightly as she watched the raven circle overhead. It had been moments since the bird had descended, but time seemed to stretch like elastic, the minutes pulling taut until they snapped into eternity. The world had gone eerily quiet—no more thunder, no more wind. Just the sound of the raven's wings cutting through the night air and the distant rustle of the forest.

Thorne was beside her, his eyes locked on the bird, his jaw clenched, a muscle twitching in his neck. There was something different about him now. Something darker. The urgency that had filled his movements earlier was gone, replaced by an unsettling stillness, as though he were waiting for something.

Or perhaps someone.

Lira's pulse quickened, her thoughts racing. She didn't know what had changed, but the pull of the raven had shifted. It was no longer the same beckoning call that had led her through the woods. Now it felt like a command, one that she was powerless to resist. Her fingers brushed the stone altar beside her, and for a brief moment, the cold of it seeped into her skin, like a warning from the earth itself.

"Thorne..." Her voice was barely a whisper, but it sliced through the thick air between them. She didn't know why she said his name, but it felt like a lifeline.

He turned toward her, his expression unreadable. For a moment, his eyes softened—just a flicker—but then the hardness returned, like a veil had dropped over him.

"Lira," he murmured, his voice strained, as though his very breath was being held back. "I need you to stay close to me. Do not move from this spot. Do you understand?"

Lira nodded, but the command in his voice made something coil uncomfortably in her stomach. It wasn't just worry that rippled through her now. It was fear. For him. For herself. For everything.

The raven above them let out a shrill call, its wings beating faster now, an unnatural rhythm. Lira took an instinctive step back, but Thorne's hand shot out, gripping her wrist with a force that sent a shockwave through her body.

"No," he said, his voice low, his face taut with a mixture of anger and something darker, more dangerous. "You don't understand. We're not alone."

The words hit Lira like a slap to the face, but before she could ask him to explain, the sound of footsteps broke through the silence. At first, it was distant, muffled by the storm that had suddenly begun to rage once again, but then it grew louder, more distinct, until it was impossible to ignore.

Lira's pulse leapt into her throat as she turned her head toward the source of the sound. There, emerging from the darkened trees, was a figure. Tall, cloaked, the edges of their robe billowing around them like shadows in the night. The raven above them cawed once more, its cry almost frantic now.

The figure stepped into the clearing, their face obscured by the hood of their cloak. But even though Lira couldn't see their face, she felt the presence of the person like a weight pressing down on her chest. Something was wrong. The air felt heavy, as if the forest itself were holding its breath.

"Thorne," the figure said, their voice cold, steady. It was a voice Lira didn't recognize, but there was a familiarity in the way it sent a chill through her bones. "I see you've found her."

Thorne's grip on Lira's wrist tightened, and she felt the tension in his body, the subtle tremor that betrayed his calm exterior. "You shouldn't be here," he said, his voice low, almost a growl. "You have no right to be."

The figure laughed, a low, unsettling sound that seemed to reverberate through the clearing. "No right? Oh, I think you'll find that I have every right, Thorne. I've been watching."

Lira's heart stuttered in her chest as she felt the weight of the stranger's words. Watching. They had been watched all along. Her pulse raced as she looked at Thorne, trying to understand what was happening. She had trusted him. She wanted to trust him. But now, in the face of this unknown threat, doubts began to creep into her mind.

"Who are you?" she asked, her voice barely above a whisper. The words felt thick in her mouth, like they didn't belong there.

The figure tilted their head slightly, as though considering her question. Then, with a smooth motion, they reached up and pulled back the hood, revealing a face that made Lira's blood run cold.

It was a woman. A woman with dark, piercing eyes that seemed to see through her, through everything. Her features were sharp, almost regal, but there was something predatory about the way she looked at Lira. Her skin was pale, almost ethereal, and her lips curled into a smile that was both chilling and knowing.

"Ah, the girl doesn't recognize me," the woman said, her smile widening. "How quaint. No matter. It's not her fault, after all."

Lira's breath caught in her throat. "Who are you?" she asked again, but this time, her voice was steady, demanding.

The woman's gaze flickered toward Thorne, a glint of something in her eyes that made Lira's stomach drop. "You really thought you could protect her, didn't you?" she said, her voice dripping with disdain. "You've always been the protector, haven't you, Thorne? But even you can't protect her from the truth."

Lira's gaze snapped to Thorne, her heart thudding painfully in her chest. "Thorne? What is she talking about? What truth?"

Thorne didn't answer immediately. He stood there, his face a mask of emotions Lira couldn't read, his jaw clenched so tightly it looked like it might snap. Finally, after what felt like an eternity, he turned to face her, his expression pained.

"I never wanted you to know," he said quietly, his voice thick with regret. "But now... I can't protect you from it anymore."

The words hit Lira like a tidal wave, and for a moment, she was paralyzed. "Protect me from what?" she whispered, her voice shaking.

Thorne's eyes softened, but there was a sadness in them now, something deeper than regret. "Lira... the curse you've been hearing—the raven's call—it's not just a call to you. It's a call to both of us."

The woman beside them laughed softly, her eyes glinting with something dark. "Oh, Thorne. You've been playing this game far too long. You think you're protecting her, but all you've done is delay the inevitable."

Lira turned to Thorne, her mind spinning. "What do you mean?" she asked, her voice breaking. "What game? What's going on?"

Thorne's gaze dropped to the ground, and for a moment, he didn't speak. Then, finally, he whispered, "I'm the one who cursed you, Lira."

The words slammed into her, ripping through her like shards of glass. She couldn't breathe. Her mind couldn't comprehend what he was saying. "No... No, that's impossible..."

But the woman smiled, a cruel smile that only deepened Lira's confusion and betrayal.

"It's true, dear," the woman said. "Thorne's bloodline has been bound to yours for generations. And now, you're bound to each other once more. The curse has always been there, waiting for this moment."

Lira shook her head, her thoughts unraveling like a frayed thread. "No," she whispered, her voice hoarse. "I don't believe you. Thorne... you..."

Thorne stepped toward her, his face strained, his eyes filled with something between sorrow and regret. But Lira couldn't bring herself to reach for him, couldn't bring herself to believe him—not now, not after everything.

The raven cried again, louder this time, the call sharp and piercing. The clearing seemed to tremble, and Lira felt the ground beneath her feet shift, the air thickening. The curse, the magic, the truth—it was all converging on this moment. And she didn't know if she was strong enough to face it.

But she had no choice.

Eight

The Song of Ravens

The night was still, the storm outside fading to a distant rumble, but the tension in the air was thick enough to suffocate. Lira stood in the clearing, the weight of Thorne's words still heavy in her chest. She hadn't moved since the truth had come crashing down on her like a wave—Thorne had cursed her. The realization had left her hollow, unable to breathe, and yet she couldn't tear herself away from him. Not yet. Not until she understood.

Her fingers, trembling despite herself, brushed against the cool stone of the altar, its surface slick with the moisture from the storm. The raven, still perched nearby, watched them intently, its eyes gleaming in the pale light as though it knew something they didn't. Its steady gaze unsettled her, but it was the quiet, almost imperceptible hum in the air that made her skin prickle. There was magic here—dark, old magic—and it was pulling at her from every direction.

Thorne was still standing near the edge of the clearing, his face unreadable, his posture tense, as though every fiber of his being was coiled with restraint. She could feel the distance between them, the emotional chasm that had opened up since the truth was revealed. The distance wasn't just physical. It was something deeper, something that felt like it had always been there, hiding just beneath the surface.

"You cursed me," Lira whispered, the words like a knife sliding through her chest.

Thorne flinched, his shoulders tensing, but he didn't turn away from her. His gaze was intense, filled with a deep, unspoken regret that tugged at something inside her. But she couldn't bring herself to feel sympathy. Not yet.

"I never wanted to," he said quietly, his voice hoarse, the words coming out ragged. "But the curse was always there, Lira. It's tied to your bloodline and mine. And there's nothing either of us can do about it. Not anymore."

Lira's breath caught in her throat, the anger bubbling up from somewhere deep inside her. She felt betrayed—more than betrayed—used. "So this was all some sort of plan, then?" she asked, her voice rising, her pulse hammering in her ears. "You cursed me to use me? For what? Some grand destiny you've been protecting me from?"

"No," Thorne said, his voice so soft it barely registered above the whisper of the wind in the trees. "This wasn't a plan. I didn't want to pull you into this. I never wanted you to be involved in any of this—but you are."

The raven cawed sharply, its wings flicking in agitation. It circled above them, diving in wide arcs around the clearing. Its call felt like an omen now, a sign of something inevitable.

Lira clenched her fists, biting back tears. "Then what am I supposed to do? What can I do?"

Thorne didn't immediately respond. Instead, he stepped closer, slowly, as though every movement required careful deliberation. When he reached her, he hesitated for a moment before extending his hand. The warmth of it sent a shiver through Lira, and against her will, she found herself drawn to him, to the magnetic pull that had always existed between them.

But she stepped back, the space between them suddenly feeling far too small.

"Please," he whispered, his voice barely audible over the wind. "Let me explain. There's a way to break the curse—but we have to understand it first."

Her breath hitched. "And how do we do that?" she asked, her voice raw.

Thorne's eyes were filled with something like sorrow, something so deep and painful that it made Lira's heart ache in spite of herself. "The raven is part of it. It's not just a symbol—it's the key to unlocking everything. The song—the one you've been hearing in your dreams—it's tied to the curse. You're the one who can break it, but only if you accept your place in this world."

Lira shook her head, the words confusing her even more. "A song?" Her voice cracked, and she clenched her fists at her sides, trying to hold onto her composure. "I've been hearing it. But I thought it was just—just some sort of…" She trailed off, the realization sinking in. "It's real."

"Yes," Thorne said, his voice low, a soft edge of urgency to it. "The song is the key, Lira. It's what binds us all together. The curse, the raven—it all comes from the same source. The song was meant to call you to it."

Lira stood in silence, the wind whispering through the trees like a secret. Her breath came in ragged gasps, each one feeling heavier than the last. She didn't know how to make sense of it. How could she? She'd spent her entire life thinking the raven was just an omen, just a story. But now… now it was more than that. It was her fate.

"Where is the song?" she asked, her voice barely a whisper. "How do I—"

Before Thorne could answer, a tremor ran through the ground, a violent shudder that sent a jolt of panic through her. The trees around them swayed violently, their branches creaking and groaning like old bones. The air seemed to hum with energy, the very fabric of the forest vibrating as though it were alive.

"The veil is weakening," Thorne said, his voice tight with alarm. "It's not safe here anymore. We have to go."

Lira opened her mouth to speak, but before she could ask another question, the raven called again—sharp and piercing, so loud it felt like it was coming from inside her skull. It echoed through the clearing, through the trees, and down into the very ground. She stumbled back, her pulse racing.

"Thorne!" she gasped. "What is happening?"

"It's beginning," Thorne said, his eyes wide with a mix of fear and determination. "The veil is opening. We're running out of time."

The raven soared downward, landing gracefully on the stone altar, its dark eyes locked onto Lira. For a moment, everything seemed to still. The wind ceased, the trees stopped moving, and Lira's breath caught in her throat. She could feel it now, the pull of the raven—stronger than ever, like a magnetic force that drew her in.

The air thickened, pressing in on her from every side. And then, in that instant of stillness, Lira heard it—the song. Soft at first, like a faint melody, a haunting lullaby that seemed to vibrate in the very air around her. It was the same song she had heard in her dreams, the same one that had pulled her to this moment, to this place. The song of the raven.

Her heart raced as the song grew louder, stronger, until it filled her mind entirely. She could feel it inside her, like it was etched into her very bones, into her blood.

And then, just as suddenly as it had started, the song stopped.

Lira gasped, her breath coming in ragged bursts as she looked around in confusion. Thorne was at her side now, his hand gripping her arm, his eyes full of urgency.

"It's time," he said, his voice hoarse. "We need to go. The veil is opening, and if we don't get to the heart of the forest, we won't be able to stop it."

Lira felt a rush of fear, but something else stirred within her—a deep, undeniable pull toward the heart of the forest. The song had called her. It had led her here.

And now, it was time to answer.

Nine

The Shattered Trust

Lira's heart pounded in her chest as she moved deeper into the forest, her footsteps muffled by the thick carpet of wet leaves and moss. The air around her was thick with the scent of rain-soaked earth and decaying wood, but there was something more—something metallic and sharp in the wind that made her skin crawl. The trees towered above her, their gnarled branches twisting like ancient fingers reaching into the dark sky. It was darker here, too dark for her to see clearly, but she didn't need to. She could feel the weight of the forest pressing in on her, the very ground beneath her feet vibrating with an energy that both terrified and exhilarated her.

Thorne was beside her, his presence solid, comforting—but there was something in his silence that gnawed at her. The words he had said just moments ago still echoed in her mind, like a dull drumbeat that refused to fade. We're running out of time. His face had been pale when he'd said it, his jaw tight with something he hadn't been willing to share. The urgency in his voice had been unmistakable, and yet, there was something else, something that felt off.

She couldn't quite place it, but every step she took felt heavier than the last. The closer they got to the heart of the forest, the more she could feel it—the veil between the worlds thinning, the magic drawing tighter around them. It was almost suffocating, the air thick with the taste of magic, of power, of something ancient that Lira wasn't ready to confront.

"Thorne," she said quietly, her voice a thread of sound in the otherwise still air. "What aren't you telling me?"

He didn't answer immediately. Instead, his eyes flickered to hers, then back to the path ahead. His lips parted as if he was about to speak, but the words never came. Lira could feel the weight of his gaze on her, but it was distant, guarded, and for the first time, she wondered if she'd ever truly known him at all.

"Thorne," she repeated, her voice growing firmer, more insistent. "Tell me the truth. What's really happening here?"

He finally stopped walking, turning to face her with a sharpness that sent a cold chill down her spine. His eyes, usually stormy but steady, now seemed hollow—lost, like there was something buried deep within them that he couldn't bear to bring to the surface. His jaw clenched, and his hands, which had been at his sides, curled into fists.

"You don't want the truth, Lira," he said, his voice strained. "Trust me. You don't."

"I already don't trust you," she shot back, the words slipping from her mouth before she could stop them. The anger bubbled up, hot and fierce, fueled by the confusion and betrayal that had been gnawing at her ever since she learned about the curse. "You lied to me. About everything. You kept me in the dark. All of this—this—was supposed to be something you were protecting me from? But you let me walk into it. You let me believe that I was in control. That I had a choice."

His eyes flashed, a flicker of something dangerous crossing his face, and for a moment, Lira thought he might lash out. But instead, he exhaled sharply, almost like a man defeated.

"I never wanted this for you," Thorne said, his voice barely above a whisper. "I never wanted you to be a part of any of it. But you were always going to be, Lira. The moment you heard the call, you were bound to it. There's no going back from that. You don't understand what's at stake here. What you're becoming."

Lira's heart stuttered in her chest, the finality of his words hitting her like a hammer. She didn't know what he meant by that—what he thought she was becoming—but she had no intention of letting him dictate what her life would be. Not anymore. Not after everything.

"What am I becoming, Thorne?" she asked, her voice trembling despite herself. "What am I?"

He stepped closer, closing the distance between them until there was barely an inch separating them. His presence was overwhelming, his warmth pulling her toward him even as his words repelled her.

"You're becoming part of the magic, Lira," he said, his voice dark, filled with a mix of regret and something else—something too sharp, too cutting for her to grasp. "A part of the forest. A part of the curse. You're bound to it in ways you can't even imagine."

Her breath caught in her throat. "What do you mean by that? Tell me what this curse is. Tell me everything."

Thorne hesitated for a long moment, as though the words he wanted to say were too dangerous to speak. Finally, he closed his eyes for a brief moment, and when he opened them again, there was something different in his gaze. Something raw, something vulnerable.

"The curse doesn't just tie our bloodlines together, Lira," he said quietly, almost to himself. "It binds us to the forest. To the ravens. To the magic that runs through the veins of this land. And when the veil opens—when the time comes—it will take everything. The price for breaking the curse is… is…" He trailed off, the words dying in his throat.

Lira stepped back, her mind racing to keep up with the flood of information, but her heart was heavy, weighing her down with every word that spilled from his lips. This wasn't just about magic. It was about them. About her.

"The price?" she repeated, her voice barely a whisper, "What price? What do you mean by that?"

He reached out, his hand brushing against hers in a fleeting moment of tenderness, but his touch felt like a burn, searing through her skin. His eyes were filled with pain—pain that mirrored her own, pain that was too much.

"You're the one who has to pay it," he said, the words coming out like a confession, like a curse itself. "The raven's song—it calls you to this moment because you're the one who must decide. You can break the curse… but at a cost. At the cost of everything you've ever known. Your life will be forever tied to the forest. To me. You will never be free."

Lira shook her head, her mind spinning, her heart racing. She could feel the weight of his words pressing on her chest, the suffocating gravity of them. And yet… there was something else, something deep within her that whispered it was true. She was bound to this. To him. To the curse.

"No," she whispered, stepping back further, her hands trembling. "I don't believe you. This isn't—this isn't my fault. You did this to me. You've been hiding everything from me, controlling me, all for some destiny that I never asked for."

Thorne's face twisted with something like guilt, something that almost looked like regret, but there was no time for it now. Lira couldn't look at him anymore. Not like this.

"You never asked for this, Lira," he said, his voice thick with emotion. "But it's always been a part of you. I've been trying to protect you from the truth—from me—but now you see it. Now you understand what you've been called to do."

The raven cawed again, sharp and piercing, its cry echoing through the night like a death knell.

"I don't understand," she said, her voice barely above a whisper, her tears burning as they slid down her cheeks. "How am I supposed to choose?"

Thorne didn't answer. Instead, he stepped away, his face dark with unresolved tension, his body taut with the weight of his own conflict.

"I don't know, Lira," he said, his voice barely a murmur. "But we're running out of time."

The ground trembled beneath them again, and the air grew heavier, thicker with the press of magic, with the promise of what was to come. Lira could feel it, could feel the curse tightening its grip around her. She didn't know what would happen next, but she knew one thing for sure.

Everything was about to change.

The Gathering Storm

The sky had darkened further, the moon veiled by thick clouds that seemed to churn with unnatural speed. The air was heavy with tension, thick with the promise of something coming. Lira could feel it in the pit of her stomach, that ever-tightening knot of unease. The world around them had gone quiet, as though even nature was holding its breath. Every snap of a twig beneath her feet, every rustle of wind through the branches seemed amplified, like the forest itself was a living, breathing thing, watching, waiting.

She walked beside Thorne, though the distance between them felt more like miles than the few steps that separated them. He had remained quiet since their argument. His silence wasn't uncomfortable so much as it was laden with unspoken words. She knew he was fighting with himself—he had told her as much. But the weight of his actions hung between them like a wall, and no amount of silence could erase the fractured trust between them.

But Lira could feel the pull of the curse, feel the song of the raven calling to her once again. It vibrated through the earth, deep and resonant, like a pulse she couldn't escape. She had to wonder whether she had always been bound to this. Whether this had been inevitable all along.

Thorne had said there was no going back. She couldn't undo what had been done. And in her heart, Lira knew he was right. She couldn't run from the darkness that was swallowing them whole, but the deeper she got into it, the more she wanted to turn away from him. Not from the feelings she had for him—those were still there, coiled tightly, waiting to be set free—but from the secret he had kept from her. From the lie she couldn't unhear.

She glanced at him now, his expression set and unreadable. His eyes were trained forward, his jaw clenched, his movements tense, like a man carrying a burden too heavy to bear. The air between them was thick with something that wasn't just the impending storm. It was a storm of their own—one neither of them could control.

"Thorne…" she said, her voice quiet but piercing in the silence that had stretched too long. "You can't keep protecting me from the truth. You can't hide it anymore."

He stiffened but didn't look at her. Instead, his gaze flickered to the edge of the trees, as though he could find some way to escape her words.

"I'm not hiding it, Lira," he said, his voice low and hoarse. "But the truth is too dangerous for you. You don't know what it will cost."

"Then let me decide!" she shot back, her voice rising despite the trepidation that fluttered in her chest. "Let me choose what happens next. I can't keep living in the dark, Thorne. I need to know everything."

He stopped walking abruptly, so sudden that Lira nearly ran into him. She looked up, but his eyes were closed, his expression tight with an emotion she couldn't read.

"It's not just your choice," he said softly, finally meeting her gaze. There was a deep sadness in his eyes—more than regret, more than guilt. It was a raw, unspoken grief. "It's the forest's choice, too. The curse binds us both, but it won't be broken without sacrifice. And it won't be easy for either of us."

Lira's breath caught in her throat. "What do you mean?"

He met her eyes, and for the first time, Lira saw the vulnerability in his gaze. He stepped closer, closing the space between them, but she didn't pull away. She could feel the heat of his body radiating toward her, the intensity in his gaze burning through the distance between them. His presence consumed her, leaving her breathless, but it wasn't just desire that heated her skin. It was the weight of everything unsaid, everything hidden.

"Lira," he whispered, his voice strained, "The curse binds us in ways that neither of us fully understand. You have to face it—we have to face it—together. There's no other way."

The words sent a shockwave through her, something she could barely comprehend. They were standing on the precipice of something so much darker than she had imagined, and yet she knew she couldn't turn away from it. She wouldn't.

"Together," she repeated, her voice a hushed breath between them.

The raven cried again, its voice shrill and sharp, the call more urgent this time, louder, piercing through the tension that surrounded them like a physical force. Lira shuddered, her hand instinctively reaching for Thorne's, but she hesitated before taking it. The magic that pulsed between them felt like a bridge between worlds, fragile, delicate, but undeniably powerful.

"We don't have much time," Thorne said, his voice urgent, as he took her hand, his grip tight, almost desperate. "We need to reach the heart of the forest, where the veil is the thinnest. Once we're there, we can try to understand how to break the curse. But…" He paused, his expression clouded with indecision. "But I don't know if we can stop what's coming. The magic is old, and it doesn't bend easily. And you…" His voice trailed off, but his eyes searched hers for something—something he couldn't say.

"I'm ready," Lira said, her voice firm despite the fluttering unease in her chest. "I'm ready to face whatever comes."

Thorne looked at her then, his eyes dark and unreadable. He seemed to search her face, as if trying to determine if she was speaking the truth or if it was just the fear talking. Finally, after a long, pregnant pause, he nodded.

"Then let's go," he said, his voice barely more than a murmur.

They walked in silence, the storm now a mere whisper in the distance, the air thick with the palpable sense of something about to break. The trees around them seemed to lean in closer, the forest becoming denser, more oppressive as they ventured deeper into its heart. The underbrush was thick with thorns and tangled roots, but Thorne guided her through it with ease, his hand never leaving hers, his presence an anchor in the midst of the chaos.

But the further they went, the more Lira felt the weight of the curse pressing in on her, the air growing heavier, as though the very forest was holding its breath. The song of the raven echoed once more, louder, clearer, until it felt like it was coming from inside her mind. She couldn't shake the feeling that it was calling her, for her. That it had always been meant for her.

The ground beneath their feet trembled slightly, a warning, and Lira stumbled, but Thorne's grip tightened around her wrist, steadying her.

"We're close," he said, his voice taut with anxiety. "Very close."

Lira nodded, but her mind was racing, her heart hammering. She didn't know what she was about to face, but she knew it would change everything. The curse, the magic, the raven's call—it was all leading them here, to this moment.

And there would be no turning back.

Eleven

The Final Flight

The forest had fallen into a suffocating silence, the kind that seemed to press in on Lira from all sides, muffling the sound of her breathing. It was as though the world had drawn in a single, collective breath and was now waiting. Waiting for the inevitable.

Thorne walked beside her, his steps sure and steady, but she could feel the tension coiling in his muscles. The air between them crackled with something dangerous, an energy so potent it made Lira's skin prickle. She kept her hand firmly in his, her pulse racing, her mind spinning with everything that had led them to this point.

They had entered the heart of the forest hours ago, pushing deeper into the shadows, where the trees grew so close together it felt like they were entering some ancient, forgotten world.

The path they followed had narrowed to a barely visible trail, and the only light now was the soft glow of bioluminescent moss at their feet and the faint flickering of lightning far in the distance.

The raven had been quiet for some time, its calls lost in the storm that seemed to follow them. Yet, the air felt alive with its presence, a quiet hum that vibrated through the ground and into their bones. Lira could feel the weight of the magic pressing against her, a presence so thick it made it hard to breathe.

Thorne squeezed her hand, his grip tight, and for a moment, their eyes met. The forest around them seemed to hold its breath.

"It's time," he said, his voice soft, but filled with an urgency that sent a shiver down her spine.

Lira nodded, her heart hammering in her chest. "What happens now?"

Thorne's lips tightened, and he drew in a slow breath before answering, as if steeling himself against something he couldn't control. "Now we face the truth. The veil is at its thinnest here. We can try to break the curse, but..." He faltered, and she could hear the hesitation in his voice.

"Thorne," Lira said, her voice a low whisper, "what aren't you telling me?"

He stopped walking then, turning to face her, and for the first time since they had entered the heart of the forest, his gaze was fully focused on her, unwavering and intense. "I've kept things from you, Lira. But it's not because I wanted to. I thought I was protecting you." He swallowed hard, his throat working. "The truth is, I'm not sure we can break the curse. The price..." His voice trailed off, and his expression shifted into something darker. "The price might be more than either of us can pay."

The words hit her like a blow to the chest, and she felt a sharp, painful tightness in her throat. For a moment, everything inside her screamed to run. To turn around and leave before it was too late. But the raven's call—a low, insistent caw—echoed in the distance, pulling her forward.

"What do you mean 'the price'?" she asked, her voice trembling despite herself.

Thorne's eyes flickered, and the moment stretched between them. His lips parted, but the words didn't come, and for a brief, fleeting second, she saw something in his eyes—something raw, something that frightened her. But before she could say anything else, the forest seemed to react, the air thickening, growing heavier.

The raven's call rang out again, this time louder, sharper, a piercing sound that seemed to tear through the stillness, resonating deep in her chest. The ground beneath them trembled, a low rumble that was not from thunder but from something beneath them.

"It's happening," Thorne said, his voice tight. "We have to move."

Without waiting for her to respond, he turned and began walking again, his pace faster now, the urgency in his steps unmistakable. Lira followed closely, her heart racing as she struggled to keep up with his long strides. The air was thick, like it was closing in on them, and Lira could feel the weight of the magic growing stronger, pressing on her chest as they moved deeper into the heart of the forest.

And then, there it was—a clearing ahead, bathed in the eerie glow of the bioluminescent moss, the trees standing like silent sentinels on all sides. At the center of the clearing was a stone archway, old and weathered, its surface covered in strange markings. The wind seemed to grow colder as they neared it, the hairs on the back of Lira's neck standing up in warning.

"This is it," Thorne whispered, his voice tight with awe and fear. "The heart of the veil. The place where the curse began."

Lira stepped forward, but before she could reach the archway, the raven appeared in the sky, its wings beating furiously as it descended toward them. It landed on a stone pillar beside the arch, its eyes glowing with an unnatural light. The bird cawed loudly, its voice cutting through the air like a blade.

The raven turned its gaze toward Lira, and for a moment, everything else faded away. It was as though time had stopped, and there was only the raven—its eyes locked onto hers, its gaze heavy with ancient knowledge.

The world seemed to shift around her, the ground beneath her feet trembling once again as a sudden gust of wind whipped through the clearing. It felt as though the forest itself was reacting to the raven's presence, and Lira could feel the air crackling with energy, the magic swirling around them like a storm.

"You have to make a choice, Lira," Thorne said, his voice strained as he stepped forward. "The curse binds you to the forest. You can either accept it—accept the power and the burden it brings— or you can try to fight it. But fighting it comes with a cost. You've felt the pull of it, the call of the raven. The magic is part of you now. You are part of it."

Lira turned to him, her heart racing. "What do you mean? What choice?"

Thorne's gaze was dark, filled with a raw, painful understanding. "If you take on the power of the curse, you'll be bound to this place forever. The forest will be yours to command, but you will never leave. The magic will run through your veins, and the raven will always watch over you. But if you try to break it—if you try to walk away—you'll lose everything. The forest will take what's most precious to you."

Lira's breath hitched in her throat. The weight of his words settled over her like a thick fog. She felt the pull of the magic deep in her chest, felt the raven's presence growing stronger, felt the power calling to her like a magnet, pulling her in. But at what cost?

Her heart wrenched in her chest as she looked at Thorne, his expression tortured, his eyes filled with regret. She wanted to reach out to him, wanted to hold him, to make sense of all of this. But the raven's call echoed in her mind again, a sharp, insistent reminder that time was running out.

The world seemed to shift around her, the air thick with magic, and for a moment, Lira couldn't tell where the forest ended and she began. She could feel the pull of it, the magic reaching for her, but she also felt Thorne's presence beside her—his warmth, his strength. He was the one constant in the storm that surrounded her.

"Thorne," she whispered, her voice breaking. "I don't know what to do."

He stepped closer, his hand reaching for hers, and when their fingers brushed, the magic between them flared to life, a surge of energy that made her heart skip. The raven watched them, its eyes glinting with something ancient, something that made her skin crawl.

"It's your choice," Thorne said softly, his voice filled with something she couldn't place. "But whatever you decide, I'll be here. I'll stand by you."

Lira closed her eyes, her breath shallow as she reached for the decision that hung in the air before her. The curse, the magic, the forest—everything had led her here. But what would be left of her when it was all over?

She opened her eyes, staring at the raven as it cawed once more. And in that moment, Lira knew. The choice had already been made.

The Ravens' Promise

The air was thick with magic, the power that bent reality itself, shaping the world around them. It swirled like a storm, coiling in the clearing where Lira stood, her body trembling as the force of it pressed against her. The trees were silent, the wind still, but the earth hummed beneath her feet, alive with an energy that made the hairs on the back of her neck stand up.

The raven perched on the stone pillar, its dark eyes locked onto hers, unblinking and unwavering. It was waiting. Waiting for her to make the final choice.

Lira's chest rose and fell with each shaky breath. The weight of everything—the curse, the magic, the forest—felt heavier than ever now. Her heart hammered in her chest, each beat thundering in her ears as she stared at the bird, the creature that had been both her guide and her prison. It had called to her, led her to this moment, and now it was asking her to choose.

Thorne stood beside her, his presence a steady anchor in the storm of her thoughts, but even his proximity couldn't calm the fire of uncertainty burning inside her. His hand brushed against hers, and she squeezed it, the touch grounding her, even as her mind raced.

"You don't have to do this," Thorne said softly, his voice barely a whisper, like he was afraid of breaking the fragile silence between them. "If you don't want this… if you can't…"

She turned to him then, her gaze meeting his, and in his eyes, she saw the fear that mirrored her own. The fear of the unknown. The fear of the price she would pay. She had no answers, no certainty, only the feeling of being trapped between two worlds, between what was right and what was necessary.

"I don't want to hurt anyone," she whispered, her voice breaking. "I just want to be free of this."

Thorne's hand tightened around hers, pulling her closer. "You have to decide, Lira. You are part of this now. But you still have the power to choose. You always have."

The raven's caw broke through the stillness, the sound sharp and insistent. It was like a signal, an urging, as if the world itself was holding its breath, waiting for her to act. Lira's throat tightened, the weight of the decision pressing on her chest, but something inside her—the magic, the bond to the forest—whispered to her. It was time.

She turned back to the raven, her heart racing as she took a tentative step forward. The creature's eyes gleamed with a knowing intelligence, and for a moment, Lira felt as though the raven was inside her, its thoughts intertwining with hers. It spoke to her without words, a message carried on the wind.

You are the key.

Her breath caught in her throat as the meaning of those words settled in her mind. The raven wasn't just a symbol. It wasn't just an omen. It was a part of her, and she was a part of it. The magic flowed through her veins, connected to the pulse of the earth, to the life of the forest. She could feel it now, stronger than ever, the weight of it, the power.

But what would it cost her?

Lira hesitated, her heart torn between two worlds. She could feel Thorne's gaze on her, a quiet plea in his eyes. He wasn't just asking her to make a choice for herself—he was asking her to make a choice for them both. They had been bound together by the curse, by the forest, by the magic. But would it break them? Would it tear them apart?

"Lira," Thorne said, his voice low but firm. "Whatever happens, whatever you choose, I'll be by your side."

His words wrapped around her like a lifeline, a tether to the only constant in this whirlwind of uncertainty. She closed her eyes, took a deep breath, and let herself feel the magic that had been building inside her all this time. The raven was the key, yes—but she was the one who held the power. The choice was hers.

Her fingers tightened around Thorne's, and in that moment, everything became clear. She wasn't just a pawn in this ancient game. She wasn't just bound to the forest by a curse. She had the power to choose her own fate.

And the power to choose his.

The raven cawed again, its call echoing through the clearing like a final warning, but Lira didn't flinch. She stepped forward, standing tall, her heart steady as she locked eyes with the bird.

"I choose," she said, her voice strong despite the trembling in her chest. "I choose to break the curse."

The forest seemed to exhale in response, the air shifting, swirling around her like a vortex of power. She could feel it in the ground beneath her feet, the pulse of the magic, the life force of the earth that was now tied to her own. The raven let out one final, piercing cry, and then, as if accepting her decision, it took flight, its wings beating through the air with an incredible force.

Lira raised her hand, her fingers outstretched, and as the raven soared above her, she felt the magic surge through her, the power of the forest flowing into her like a tide, wrapping around her like a cloak, binding her to the land and to the magic that ran through it. She gasped, her body shuddering with the force of it, but she didn't pull away. She didn't run. She embraced it.

The curse was breaking.

But at what cost?

Thorne's hand was still in hers, his grip unrelenting, and for a moment, as the magic swirled around them, Lira turned to him, her eyes meeting his with a mix of fear and something else—something deeper, something she couldn't name.

"I did it," she whispered, her voice raw. "I chose."

Thorne's face was pale, his eyes wide as he watched the magic around them, the power of it. The storm had passed, the winds died down, and in the stillness that followed, there was a strange peace—a fragile calm that hung in the air.

But then, as the magic began to settle, something in the distance caught Lira's eye. A shadow, darker than the night itself, moving quickly through the trees. And in that moment, she knew. The battle wasn't over.

It had only just begun.

"Thorne," she whispered, her voice trembling with realization. "It's not done. It's not over yet."

The look on Thorne's face was all too familiar—a look of regret, of something unsaid. "I'm sorry, Lira," he said, his voice filled with a sorrow that cut through her like a blade. "This is just the beginning."

The forest seemed to hold its breath once more as the shadow in the distance grew larger, closer. And with it, a promise—the promise of a fight that neither of them was prepared for.